The INSIDE GUIDE

STEM IN SPORTS

STEM in Football

By Beatrice Harris

Cavendish Square

Published in 2025 by Cavendish Square Publishing, LLC
2544 Clinton Street Buffalo, NY 14224

Website: cavendishsq.com

Disclaimer: Portions of this work were originally authored by Ryan Nagelhout and published as *The Science of Football* (Sports Science). All new material this edition authored by Beatrice Harris.

All websites were available and accurate when this book was sent to press.

Library of Congress Cataloging-in-Publication Data

Names: Harris, Beatrice, author.
Title: STEM in football / Beatrice Harris.
Description: Buffalo, New York : Cavendish Square Publishing, [2025] |
Series: The inside guide: STEM in sports | Includes index.
Identifiers: LCCN 2023050095 (print) | LCCN 2023050096 (ebook) | ISBN 9781502671370 (library binding) | ISBN 9781502671363 (paperback) | ISBN 9781502671387 (ebook)
Subjects: LCSH: Football–Juvenile literature. | Science–Study and teaching–Juvenile literature. | Sports sciences–Juvenile literature.
Classification: LCC GV950.7 .H365 2025 (print) | LCC GV950.7 (ebook) | DDC 796.332–dc23/eng/20231101
LC record available at https://lccn.loc.gov/2023050095
LC ebook record available at https://lccn.loc.gov/2023050096

Editor: Therese Shea
Copyeditor: Danielle Haynes
Designer: Deanna Lepovich

The photographs in this book are used by permission and through the courtesy of: Cover, pp. 4, 10 JoeSAPhotos/Shutterstock.com; p. 6 sirtravelalot/Shutterstock.com; p. 8 Robert Nyholm/Shutterstock.com; p. 9 jjaf/Shutterstock.com; p. 12 oasisamuel/Shutterstock.com; p. 13 Brad McPherson/Shutterstock.com; p. 14 Mark Herreid/Shutterstock.com; p. 15 OSTILL is Franck Camhi/Shutterstock.com; p. 16 UPI/Alamy Stock Photo; p. 18 Steve Jacobson/Shutterstock.com; pp. 19, 28 (bottom) Gorodenkoff/Shutterstock.com; p. 20 (graph elements) Anshuman Rath/Shutterstock.com; p. 20 (graph football) Vectorpocket/Shutterstock.com; p. 21 Pete Saloutos/Shutterstock.com; p. 22 Danny E Hooks/Shutterstock.com; pp. 24, 28 (top) Joseph Sohm/Shutterstock.com; p. 25 Lev Malevich/Shutterstock.com; p. 26 tishomir/Shutterstock.com; p. 27 MPH Photos/Shutterstock.com; p. 29 (top) Margaret Kite/Shutterstock.com; p. 29 (bottom) Mike Liu/Shutterstock.com.

Some of the images in this book illustrate individuals who are models. The depictions do not imply actual situations or events.

CPSIA compliance information: Batch #CSCSQ25: For further information contact Cavendish Square Publishing LLC at 1-877-980-4450.

Printed in the United States of America

CONTENTS

Physics is the science of matter and energy and how they interact. It can explain running, passing, blocking, and kicking plays in football.

A STEM SPORT

Chapter One

Football games are filled with exciting plays, such as spiraling passes, superfast runs, and long, precise kicks. Football is a sport that any spectator can enjoy, but fans might start to examine the action more closely and have questions. Why do some kicks and passes make it down the field while others don't? Does the weather affect play? Why is the football the odd shape it is instead of round?

You can answer all these questions and more with STEM knowledge! STEM stands for science, **technology**, engineering, and math.

Fast Fact

In some countries, soccer is called football. The kind of football played in the National Football League (NFL) is sometimes called American football in these countries. There are other types of football too.

Terms for Forces and Motion

Physics explains forces and motion, which are both important parts of football. A force is a push or pull on an object. The push or pull comes from an interaction with another object. When that interaction stops, the force stops. In football, examples of force can be found all over the field—from a ball falling into the hands of a **wide receiver** to a **defensive back** trying to pull that ball away.

Two common forces displayed in football are applied force and friction. Applied force is when one object applies a force to another object. In football, that could mean tackling another player or throwing a ball, for example. A force of resistance is called friction. Friction tries to stop two objects from sliding over each other. A player's shoes supply friction against the surface of the field so the player doesn't slip. Friction between a rolling ball and the grass makes the ball stop.

The physics terms speed, velocity, and acceleration can apply to football, too, but announcers tend to use them incorrectly. The chart on the next page shows their different meanings. For example, a **running back** might run as fast as 20 miles (32 kilometers) per hour. That's speed.

Linemen try to supply enough force to keep opponents from reaching their quarterback.

To report velocity, you'd need to add direction, such as 20 miles per hour east. For the player to truly accelerate, their velocity needs to change.

physics term	what it means	equation
speed	how fast an object moves over time	speed = distance/time
velocity	an object's change in position over time plus its direction	velocity = **displacement**/time
acceleration	the change in an object's velocity over time plus its direction	acceleration = change in velocity/ time

If a football player runs from one place to another and then back at a speed of 20 miles per hour, their displacement is 0 because their overall position didn't change. That means their velocity is 0 too!

Fast Fact

The force of a hit depends on body mass, speed, and acceleration.

Hard Hitting

Forces contribute to football's possible dangers. Equipment is needed for safety. Equipment is an example of how engineering and technology impact a football game.

Hard hits are a part of every NFL game. Scientists say an average-sized defensive back weighing 199 pounds (90 kilograms) can create 1,600 pounds (726 kg) of force! They estimate the human body can handle a hit twice as hard as that, as long as the force of the hit is distributed, or spread out, throughout the body.

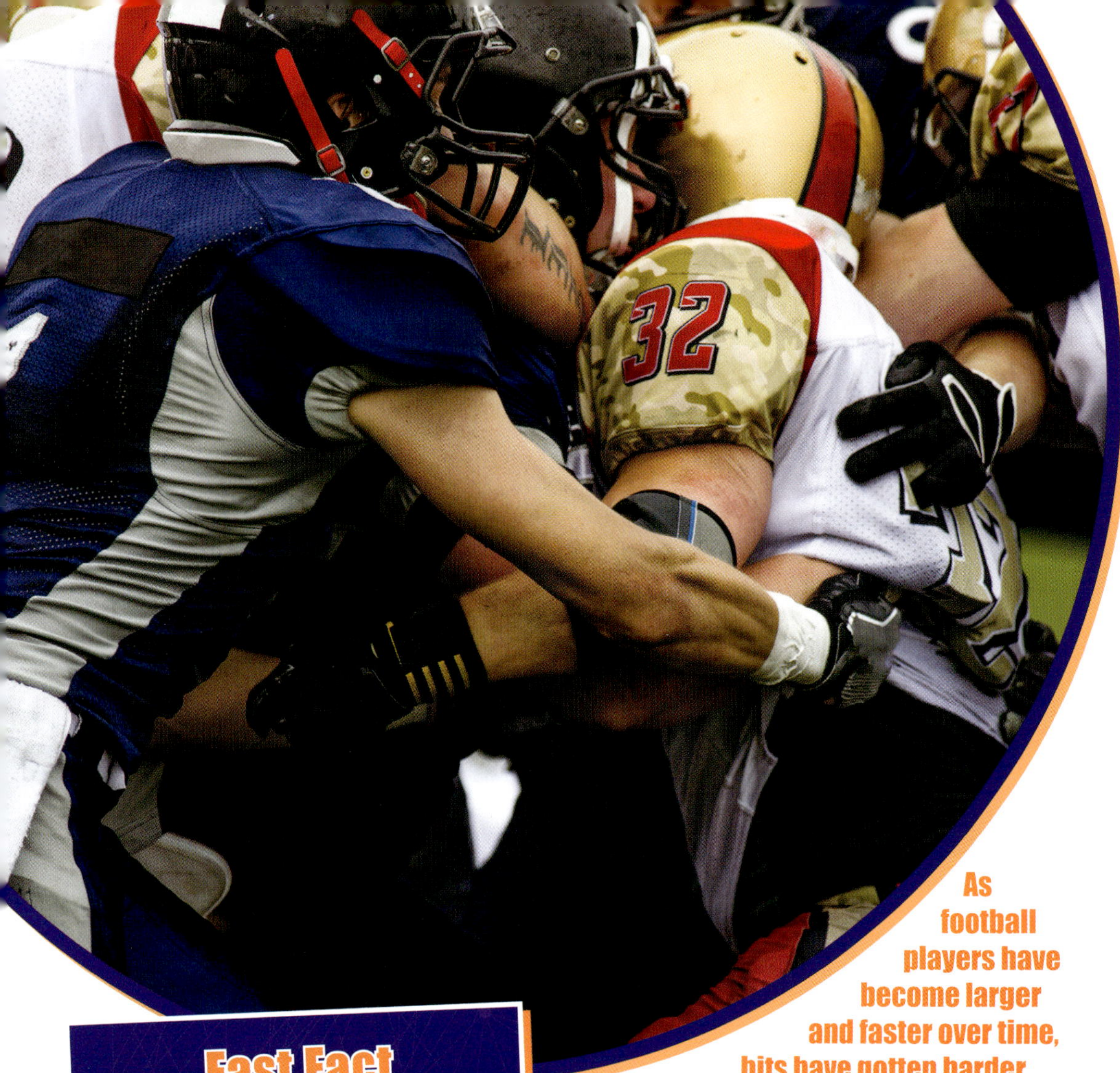

As football players have become larger and faster over time, hits have gotten harder.

Fast Fact

Engineers have figured out how to make football pads thinner and lighter than they once were. The pads still protect players, but they don't slow players down as much as heavier pads do.

The equipment players wear—including pads and helmets—are made from special hard plastic and foam that's engineered to distribute a hit's force evenly.

HEAD INJURIES

Scientists and football players recognize the link between hits and brain injuries. Although helmets are still important, they don't stop a player's head from hitting another object, such as another player or the ground. Within the helmet, the brain can bang against the skull, resulting in a brain injury called a concussion. Studies have also shown that even non-concussive injuries can lead to brain damage. The NFL is employing some measures to make the game safer, such as making helmet-to-helmet contact illegal. It is also partnering with research universities who will study the data collected by mouthguard sensors worn during games to learn more about the hits players take.

New helmet technology may help reduce the number of concussions in pro football in the future.

Geometry is the branch of math that has to do with shapes and measurements. The geometry of a football affects how the game is played.

THE FEATURES OF A FOOTBALL

Chapter Two

People who grow up watching and playing football may not question the ball's shape. However, a football's unique shape makes this sport **unpredictable** and exciting.

All in the Shape

A football's shape is a prolate spheroid. That's a rounded shape longer than it is wide. It's this "squashed" form that allows a player to tuck the ball under their arm. A sphere would be more likely to pop out and result in a **fumble**.

A prolate spheroid moves differently than a round ball does when it bounces. It's tough to predict how a football will bounce because of its shape. When a player fumbles the football, there's no telling where it will go. Fans hold their breath as they watch. Sometimes it bounces right back to the ball carrier. Other times, it bounces away, into the arms of an opponent.

Fast Fact

The first footballs were made from pigs' bladders, which gave them their odd shape. They kept this shape even after they began to be made from other materials, such as leather and rubber.

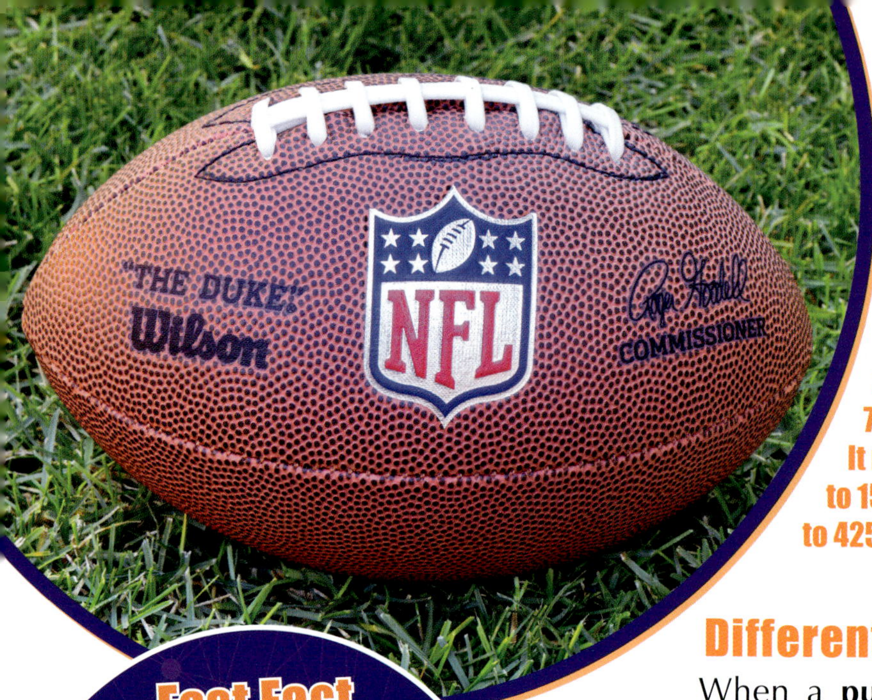

An NFL football must be 11 to 11.25 inches (27.9 to 28.6 centimeters) long and 28 to 28.5 inches (71 to 72.4 cm) around. It must weigh 14 to 15 ounces (397 to 425 grams).

Different Kicks

> **Fast Fact**
>
> Aerodynamics is the study of the way air moves around objects. Aerodynamics tells us a thrown football travels straighter if it's spinning around its long axis, which is the imaginary line that goes longways through the football.

When a **punter** kicks the ball, they drop it onto the top of their foot. However, a **placekicker** uses the side of their foot. Placekickers didn't always do this, though. They once used the top of their foot too. Later, placekickers realized they could control the ball much better and kick it farther if they kicked it like a soccer player.

Soccer-style kicks start by a player approaching the ball from the side. This allows the hip to rotate, which creates more foot speed and force to move the ball. It also gives the kicker more surface area to hit the ball with because they use the inside part of the foot.

The ball then follows a parabolic arc. This is a U-shaped curve that a thrown object, or projectile, follows because of gravity.

The punter kicks the ball downfield to the receiving team.

CONNECTING WITH K-BALLS

Kickers and punters use different footballs. The NFL added "K-balls" to the game in 1999 because kickers were doing things to the regular footballs to make them go higher and farther. Kickers would try to soften the leather and add more air to the ball. K-balls come right out of the box before the game, so they are hard, and players have little time to soften them. The balls have a waxy top layer, which makes them slippery, reducing friction needed for control. Kickers rub them on the field to break down the waxy layer and soften the leather.

Kickers need to get the ball far down the field, so they do what they can do to make the ball as aerodynamic as possible.

The football follows this course with speed and distance. At the highest point of the parabola, the ball reaches its maximum height and speed. It begins to fall due to the force of gravity. The greater the force of the kick, the higher the highest point will be and the farther the ball will travel.

> **Fast Fact**
>
> In the NFL, the average hang time for a kickoff is 4.4 seconds. Some NFL punters can achieve hang times of 5 seconds.

The ball travels farthest when kicked at an angle of 45 degrees. It travels highest—and will stay in the air longest—when kicked at a 90-degree angle. This hang time in the air is important because it allows the team on defense to prepare to stop the receiving team once a player catches the ball.

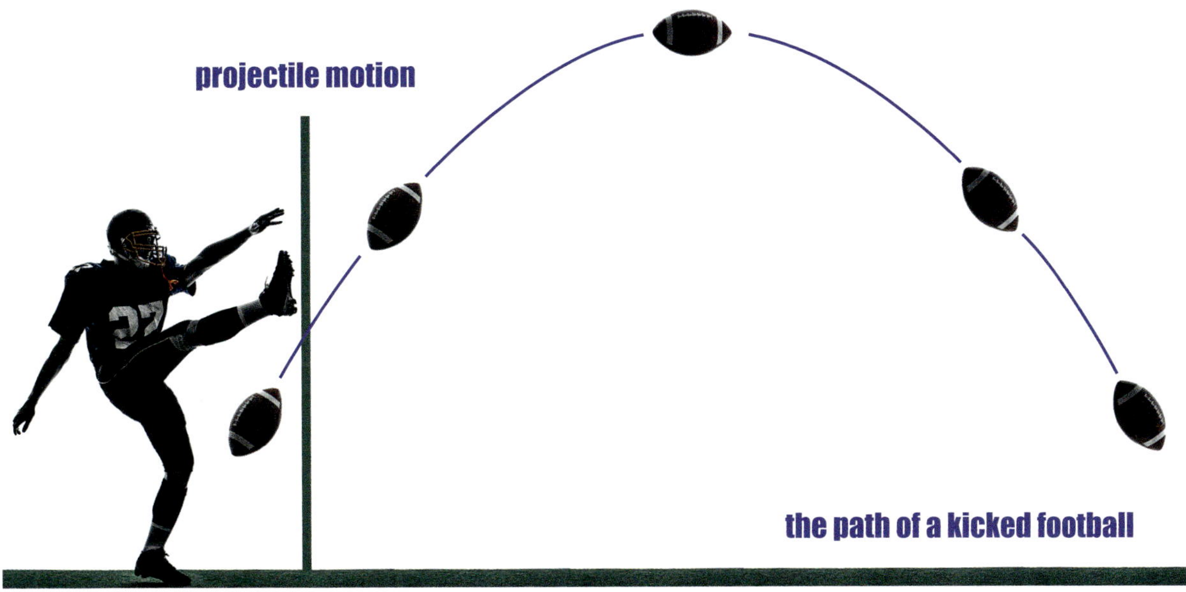

In an actual game, a ball couldn't travel in a perfect parabola because of forces such as air resistance and wind.

Perhaps the most famous position in football is quarterback. Quarterbacks such as Patrick Mahomes are team leaders.

THROWS AND CATCHES

Chapter Three

The quarterback is often the player calling the plays on offense and is the one doing most of the passing, or throwing. A quarterback's greatest rival might not be another player or team but the force called gravity!

What Goes Up

Gravity is the force that makes objects fall to Earth. Three things determine how far a football goes as gravity tries to pull it back to Earth: the force with which it's thrown, the angle it's thrown at, and the rotation, or spinning, of the ball.

If you follow the path of the ball from the quarterback to the receiver, you see that passes create a parabola too. When quarterbacks throw the football harder, their passes follow a straighter line. However, balls that make a higher parabolic shape can drop over a defender and into the waiting arms of a wide receiver.

Fast Fact

A well-thrown football makes about 600 rotations per minute!

The Spiral

Quarterbacks throw the football down the field so that it rotates around its axis toward its target.

Quarterbacks like Josh Allen must decide what path they want their pass to take. Then, they must use the right amount of force to get the ball to take that course. They only have seconds to do this.

This is called a spiral. While some think the spiral makes the ball go farther, that's not true. The ball would actually go farther and faster without any spiral motion. However, the throw is much more accurate, or exact, with the spiral. The position of the ball remains the same throughout its flight, and it experiences less air resistance than a ball tumbling end over end. A spiraling ball is also much easier to catch.

Incredible Catches

Isaac Newton was a scientist who published three basic laws of motion in 1687. We can see

METEOROLOGY MATTERS

Meteorology is the branch of science that has to do with conditions in Earth's atmosphere. People call these conditions weather. Weather can cause headaches at football games. Wind acts as a force to send footballs off course. The slower the football and the higher the wind speed, the greater the chance the football will go someplace other than its intended target. Winds going against the direction of the ball push back the ball. What makes matters more complicated is that wind speeds at ground level can be much less powerful than those 30 feet up (9 meters), where a kicked ball travels.

Rain can impact a football, making the ball heavier and reducing how far it can travel. Football players learn how to adjust their play to different conditions.

Newton's laws of motion at work in football. The first law explains that an object—such as a football on the ground—will not move without an applied force. It also says that an object in motion, such as a thrown football, will continue in the same direction and at the same speed if no other forces are acting on it. Of course, plenty of forces are acting

Fast Fact

Newton's third law of motion is in play with a tackle. The two players exert equal and opposite forces on each other as they come to a stop.

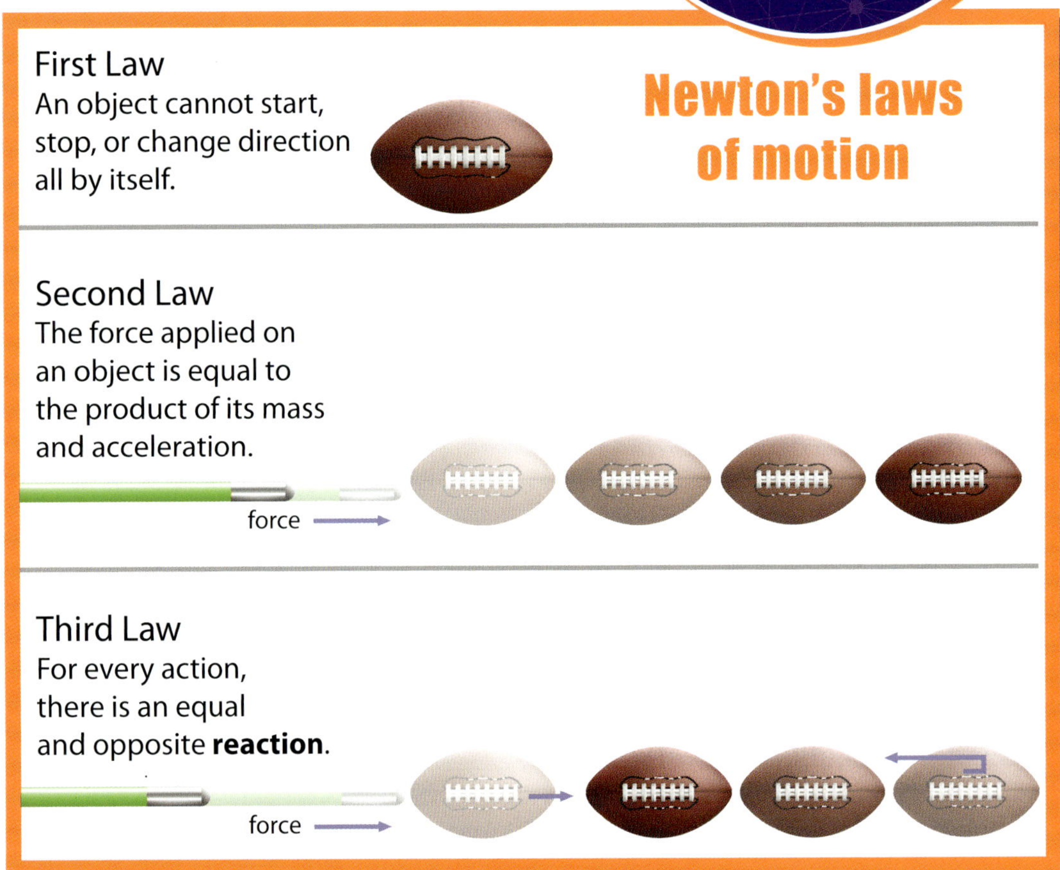

Isaac Newton's three laws of motion can be applied to all sports.

Fast Fact

Receivers want to increase the friction between the ball and their hands so they can catch it more easily. They wear special gloves for this purpose.

College and pro players can make hard catches look easy! They're used to the physical forces of the field.

on a football in the air, including gravity and air resistance.

The second law helps us figure out the force of a football when it's thrown down the field by a quarterback. The force equals the mass of the football multiplied by the acceleration of the football.

The third law of motion can be applied to a receiver in football catching the quarterback's throw. It states that each action has an equal and opposite reaction. So, a thrown ball will exert, or apply, a force on the receiver and the receiver will exert an equal and opposite force on the ball with the catch.

American football fields are 100 yards (91 m) from goal line to goal line. Each yard is marked on the field. One yard is equal to 3 feet (0.9 m).

ONTO THE FIELD

Chapter Four

The skill of the players makes a huge difference in a football game. However, other factors are at play, too, as you've read. Now, let's talk turf, or the surface of the field.

Artificial or Real?

You might think the grass on your front lawn is the same as the kind used on football fields, but it's likely not. Different kinds of grasses grow in different areas of the country, and grasses such as turfgrass are great for football fields. People who care for this grass need to know a lot about the science of plant growth. Football fields need lots of water and care to stay in good shape during a long season.

> **Fast Fact**
>
> Some NFL stadiums have a retractable roof. That means it can be pulled back. The home team decides if the roof will be open or closed before the game. Officials can decide to close it during the game if the weather is bad.

Beginning in the 1960s, the technology called artificial turf became popular in many football stadiums. This engineered material didn't need water and sunlight or

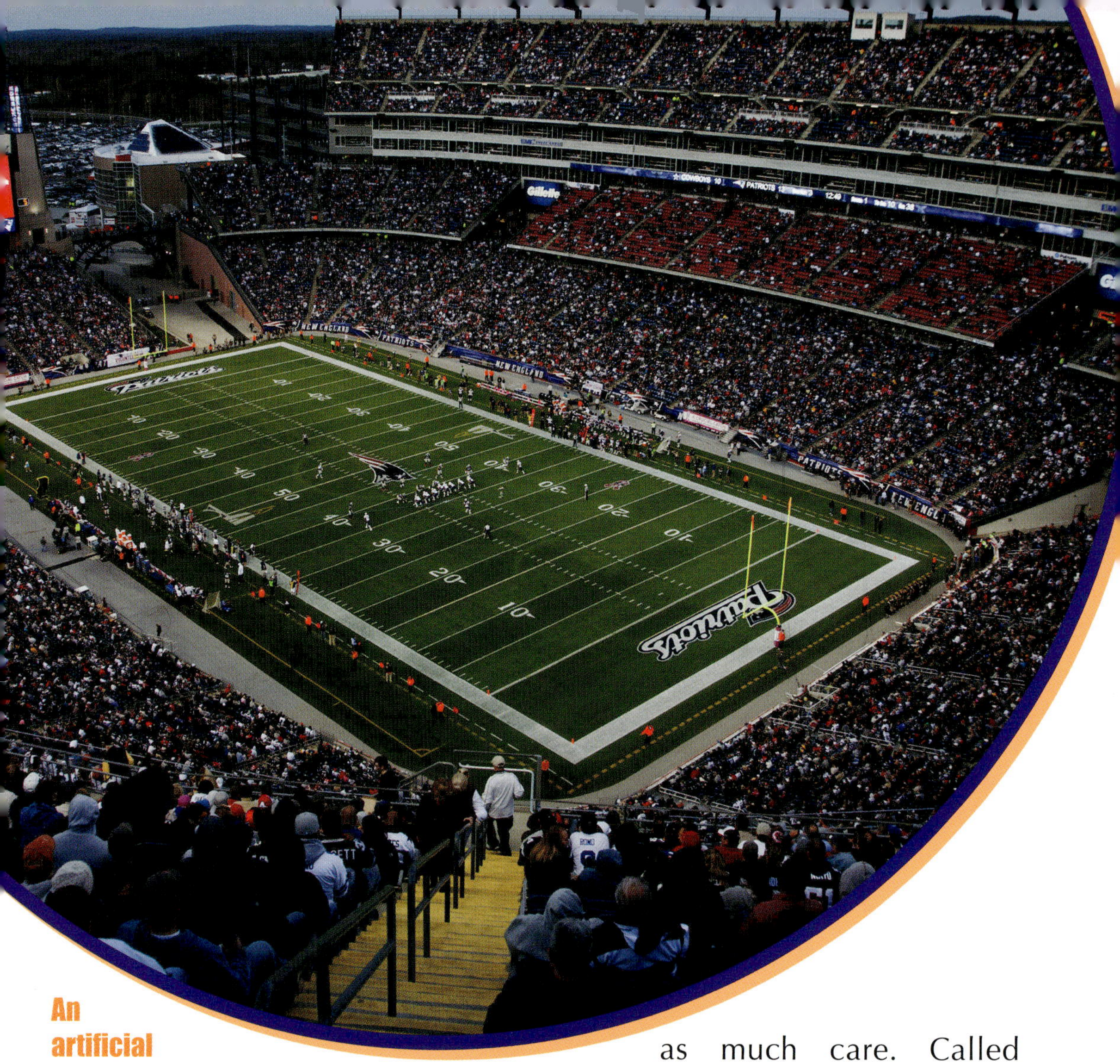

An artificial turf called FieldTurf is used at the stadiums of the Atlanta Falcons, New York Giants (and New York Jets), and New England Patriots.

as much care. Called AstroTurf, the green, carpet-like material was laid over concrete. Astroturf has since been replaced by more advanced artificial turfs that look and feel more like real grass. Individual blades of artificial grass, sand, and even extra padding between the turf and concrete are used to help prevent injuries.

DOES THE TURF MAKE A DIFFERENCE?

Even with artificial turf technology changing over the decades, playing on artificial turf feels different than playing on grass. Many players report that artificial turf—and the solid ground beneath it—is tougher on their bodies. They say grass would help absorb some of the forces their bodies experience. They blame the turf for certain injuries. The ball also bounces differently on artificial turf since it's a harder surface than it would on grass. The NFL Players Association has requested that the league change all stadium fields back to natural grass surfaces.

This is an up-close look at a kind of artificial turf. Small pieces of rubber provide cushioning, but some don't think that's enough to prevent injury.

The Arizona Cardinals play in a stadium with cool technology. To make sure the field gets enough sun, the grass grows in a tray on large tracks that lead in and out of the stadium, where it sits outside until needed.

The Air Up There

The Denver Broncos' field is just outside of Denver, Colorado. It's called Mile High Stadium because Denver is located in the mountains, about 1 mile (1.6 km) above sea level. Many football players say it's a tough place to play because of the "thin" Colorado air. There's truth to that.

Air becomes less **dense** at higher elevations. That means there's less oxygen in the air in Denver than in another NFL city such as Jacksonville, Florida, which is about 16 feet (5 m) above sea level. Less oxygen can lead to shortness of breath and a faster heartbeat, but Broncos players' bodies are used to the conditions.

Fast Fact

Kickers and punters in Denver can kick the ball farther because there are fewer air molecules and less air resistance to slow it down.

Cheers for STEM!

Players say that playing on their home field is an advantage. Part of that is the home crowd cheering them on. A decibel (dB) is a unit used to measure sound level. NFL stadiums can get very loud. How loud? Normal talking is around 60 dB. An NFL stadium's noise can exceed 130 dB!

In the crowd and on the field, STEM is at work at every football game. Players use knowledge of science, especially biology and physics, to train. Technology such as video helps coaches and officials review the action. Stadiums were built by engineers. Math is needed to keep score and for team and player **statistics**. Knowing STEM can take football to the next level for both fans and players!

Fast Fact

The Kansas City Chiefs' Arrowhead Stadium in Kansas City, Missouri, is the loudest in the NFL. A record 142.2 dB was recorded there in 2014.

Any noise over 120 dB can cause hearing damage right away, so you might want to wear ear protection at a football game in a loud stadium, such as the stadium where the Seattle Seahawks play.

THINK ABOUT IT!

1. How is your favorite part of football affected by STEM?

2. Think of a way that a STEM idea could make a player's performance better.

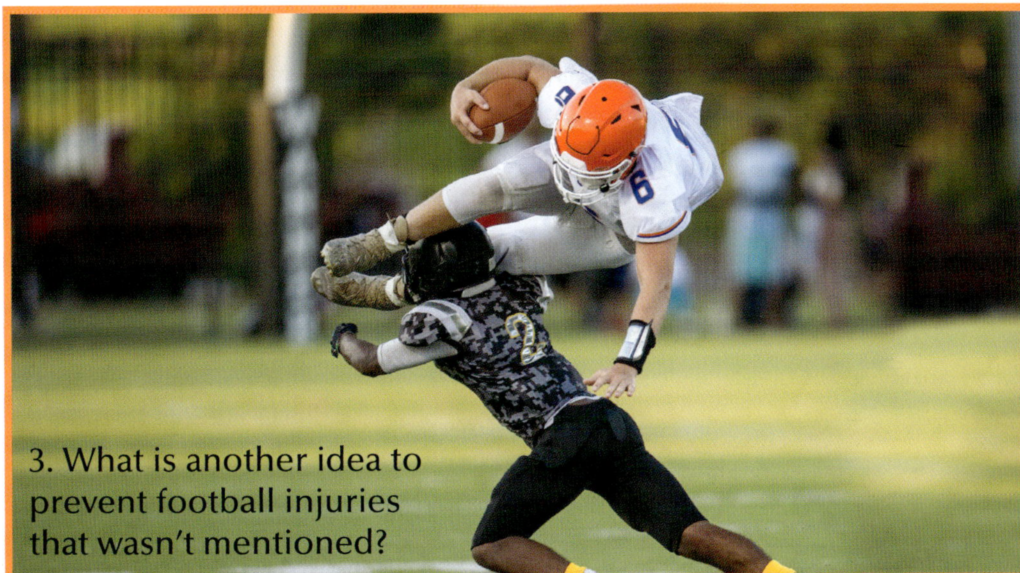

3. What is another idea to prevent football injuries that wasn't mentioned?

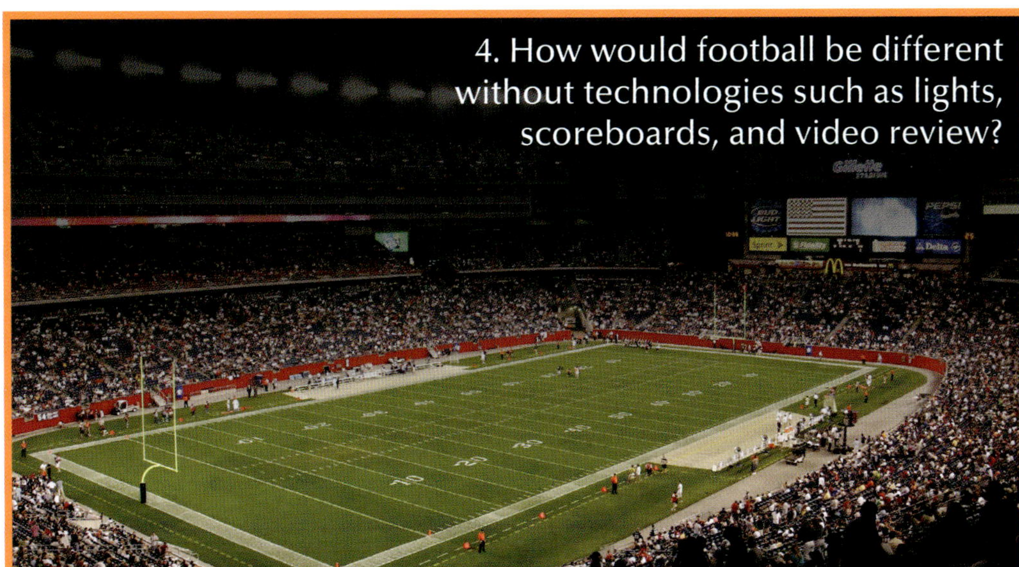

4. How would football be different without technologies such as lights, scoreboards, and video review?

GLOSSARY

defensive back: A football player responsible for defending against the wide receiver. Defensive backs include cornerbacks and safeties.

dense: Packed very closely together.

displacement: The movement of an object from its original position.

fumble: To drop the football while it is still in play.

kickoff: The action of a football player kicking the ball down the field at the start of each half, after a touchdown, and after a successful field goal.

placekicker: In football, the player who kicks field goals, extra points, and kickoffs.

punter: In football, the kicker who kicks the ball to the opponent during their team's fourth down. They try to kick the ball to a far field position but cannot kick it into the end zone.

reaction: The force that an object subjected to an outside force exerts in the opposite direction.

running back: A football player who specializes in carrying the ball up the field.

statistics: Information that can be related in numbers.

technology: Using science, engineering, and other industries to invent useful tools or to solve problems. Also, a machine, piece of equipment, or method created by technology.

unpredictable: Not capable of being known before happening.

wide receiver: An offensive football player who tries to get open to catch a pass from the quarterback.

FIND OUT MORE

Books

Flynn, Brendan. *Football*. Minneapolis, MN: A&D Xtreme, 2023.

George, Enzo. *Physical Science in Football*. St. Catharines, Ontario: Crabtree Publishing Company, 2020.

Kelley, K. C. *Football: Score with STEM!* Minneapolis, MN: Bearport Publishing Company, 2022.

Websites

Football: Rules
www.ducksters.com/sports/footballrules.php
Review the basic rules of American football.

How NFL Equipment Works
entertainment.howstuffworks.com/fb-equip.htm
Read about the kinds of gear needed to keep a pro footbal team safe.

How the Physics of Football Works
entertainment.howstuffworks.com/physics-of-football.htm
Learn more about how science affects the action on the field.

Publisher's note to educators and parents: Our editors have carefully reviewed these websites to ensure that they are suitable for students. Many websites change frequently, however, and we cannot guarantee that a site's future contents will continue to meet our high standards of quality and educational value. Be advised that students should be closely supervised whenever they access the internet.

INDEX